indonesian
desserts & snacks

William Wongso and Hayatinufus A. L. Tobing

PERIPLUS

Essential Ingredients

Adzuki beans: Small, red dried beans which must be soaked before using. Very popular in Asian sweets and readily available from Asian food stores.

Banana leaves: Used to wrap a wide selection of both sweet and savory cakes. After stripping the leaf from its hard center stem, the leaves are "softened" by being dipped for 5 to 10 seconds in boiling water or passed over a flame for a few seconds. This makes them pliable and easy to work with as fresh leaves are stiff and tear easily. The leaves need to be cut into squares or rectangles for wrapping—the specific sizes are given in the individual recipes. For aesthetic reasons, cakes are usually wrapped with the glossy side of the leaf on the outside and the matte underside on the inside.

Chilies: Red (ripe) and green (unripe) finger-length chilies are used in Indonesian snacks, as are the very hot, tiny birds eye chilies (red bird's eye chilies are usually used as opposed to other bird's eye chilies). As with all chilies, discard seeds for reduced heat and wear rubber gloves to protect your skin if you are not used to handling chilies; always wash your hands carefully afterwards.

Cinnamon: Powdered cinnamon is used occasionally in Indonesian snacks and desserts and is readily available from Asian food stores in powder form. It can also be made by grating or grinding pieces of cinnamon stick.

Coconut milk: To obtain fresh thick coconut milk, add 125 ml ($1/2$ cup) water to the grated flesh of one coconut and squeeze. To obtain fresh thin coconut milk, squeeze the grated flesh with another 625 ml ($2^1/2$ cups) water. Packaged coconut milk is readily available in large supermarkets and Asian food stores.

Fennel: Fennel seeds taste similar to aniseed. The seeds resemble cumin seeds in appearance but can easily by identified by their aroma and flavor.

Flour: Various types of flour are used in Indonesian cakes and desserts, most notably rice flour, glutinous rice flour and tapioca flour. All are available from Asian food stores.

Kaffir lime leaf: The double leaf of the kaffir lime is very fragrant and is used, whole or finely shredded, in some Padang dishes.

Lemon basil: A variety of Southeast Asian basil with a distinct lemony aroma. Lemon basil leaves are slightly smaller than European, or sweet, basil and are paler green and often more hairy.

Lemongrass: Only use the thicker bottom one third of the stem, and remove any dried outer leaves. Dried lemongrass is available but it is better to use the fresh variety.

Palm sugar: Made from either the aren or coconut palm, this raw sugar has a wonderfully rich flavor. Substitute with dark brown sugar or maple syrup.

Pandan leaves: Used to impart a delicate scent to cakes, pandan (or screwpine) leaves are sometimes cut into lengths and enclosed in a parcel. Otherwise, they may be torn into shreds lengthwise and tied into a knot. A pandan knot is usually slipped into a mixture or steamed with glutinous rice to allow its fragrance to be released. Pandan leaves used this way are always removed before serving. Sometimes when a cake requires both fragrance and a delicate shade of green, pandan essence is extracted by grinding the leaves to a pulp. The juice is strained before being added to a cake batter or dough. Traditionally, this would be done with a granite mortar and pestle but in modern kitchens, the electric blender or chopper provides a much more convenient alternative.

Rice flour: Made from ground long grain rice is used to make dough and batter in many Asian desserts.Fresh rice flour was traditionally made by soaking rice overnight and grinding it slowly in a stone mill. The same result may be achieved by grinding soaked rice in blender. Dried rice flour is available in supermarkets and provision shops, as is **glutinous rice flour** made from sticky glutinous rice.

Nutmeg: Indigenous to eastern Indonesia—the Spice Islands—nutmeg is a nut covered by a shiny, hard shell. Inside the shell, and covering the nutmeg is mace, a shiny red lacey web. Dried nutmeg keep almost indefinitely and should be grated or crushed just before using.

Slaked lime water: .Can be purchased from grocers and market stalls. It looks not unlike milk of magnesia: a white grainy powder that settles to the bottom of the container, with a clear liquid above. It should be well shaken before use. Added sparingly to batters and doughs, slaked lime water is used to improve the texture of certain cakes. Fritter batters retain their crispness longer, glutinous rice flour doughs take on a more springy texture.

Double-wrapped banana leaf packet

The banana leaf is a versatile material that is widely used in preparing Indonesian dishes. It is frequently used to wrap food for grilling, steaming, or grilling directly over hot coals. Almost any type of meat, such as duck, chicken, beef and even eels, can be chopped, seasoned and wrapped in banana leaves to be cooked.

To use, first wipe the banana leaf clean and cut it to the required sizes. Dip it in boiling water or heat it directly over a gas flame until it softens enough to be pliable without cracking. If banana leaves are not available, aluminum foil can be used, though it does not impart the subtle flavors that banana leaves do

Large pieces of banana leaf as main wrappers
Small strips of banana leaf for outer wrapping
1 quantity Filling
Wok with cover and steaming rack or steamer set

Step 1: Cut the large banana leaf wrappers into 20 x 22 cm (8 x 9 in) sheets. Cut the small banana leaf strips into 5 x 20 cm (2 x 8 in) strips. Place the required amount of Filling in the center of a large banana leaf wrapper.

Step 2: Pleat one side of the wrapper with your index finger and bring the two resulting edges of the leaf together as shown to form "wings".

Step 3: Repeat with the other side of the wrapper.

Step 4: Fold one wing of each pleat on the left and right to the front of the package.

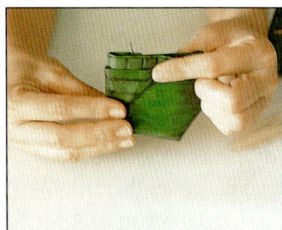

Step 5: Fold the wings on the reverse side to the back of the package.

Step 6: Place the package in the center of a smaller strip of banana leaf and fold up to hold the pleats together

Step 7: Secure with a toothpick.

Step 8: Tuck in any open corners and prepare for steaming. Fill a wok or steamer with water to a depth of 5 cm (2 in). Bring the water to a boil. Place the packages on the steamer rack set inside the wok or steamer. Cover the wok or steamer and cook for 35 minutes, adding more boiling water every 10 minutes or as needed.

Spicy Flaked Tuna Rice Packets

500 g ($2^1/_2$ cups) glutinous rice, washed and
soaked overnight
1 pandan leaf, tied in
a knot
1 teaspoon salt
200 ml ($^3/_4$ cup) thin
coconut milk
Banana leaves, softened
and cut into 25 pieces
(16 x 20 cm/ $6^1/_2$ x 8 in)

Filling
500 g (1 lb) fresh tuna,
gutted and cleaned
2 tablespoons lime juice
$^1/_2$ teaspoon salt
3–4 red chilies, sliced
5 *chili padi* (bird's-eye
chilies)
1 stalk lemongrass (inner
part only), sliced
2 cm ($^3/_4$ in) ginger,
roughly chopped
2 cloves garlic chopped
4 tablespoons oil
1 pandan leaf, finely
shredded
200 ml ($^3/_4$ cup +
1 tablespoon) thick
coconut milk
20 lemon basil leaves,
finely shredded
$^1/_4$ teaspoon salt
1 teaspoon sugar

Makes 25 pieces
Preparation time: **1 hour**
Cooking time: **40 mins**

1 To make the Filling, rub the fish with salt and lime juice. Set aside for 15 minutes. Steam until fish is firm and cooked, about 20 minutes. When cool enough to handle, remove meat and flake finely to yield 225 g (8 oz) flaked meat. Discard the head, skin and bones.
2 Grind chilies, lemongrass, ginger and garlic until smooth. Heat oil and fry the mixture until fragrant and oil separates. Add the shredded pandan leaf and stir-fry for one minute or until wilted. Add the flaked fish and coconut milk. Cook over medium heat, stir-ring continuously until most of the liquid evaporates and Filling becomes quite dry. Stir in the shredded lemon basil, salt and sugar, cook for another minute and remove pan from the heat. Set aside to cool.
3 Drain glutinous rice and place in a shallow heat-proof container, burying the pandan leaf in the rice. Steam over rapidly-boiling water for 15 minutes.
4 Add salt to the coconut milk and stir until it is dissolved. Pour into the partially-cooked rice and stir with a wooden spoon until all the coconut milk is absorbed into the rice. Continue steaming for another 20 minutes or until rice is completely cooked. Discard pandan knot.
5 Place 3 tablespoons of glutinous rice on a pre-cut banana leaf and spread it out evenly, 1 cm ($^1/_2$ in) thick. Place 1 tablespoon of filling in a line along the center of the rice. Roll up each banana leaf tightly to enclose the rice and Filling. Secure each end of the banana leaf with a toothpick.
6 Brush each packet lightly with oil and grill over charcoal. Alternatively, place as many packets as will fit snugly in a frying pan and cook over low heat for 3 to 4 minutes on each side. Serve warm.

The Spicy Flaked Tuna Rice Packets may be prepared in advance and stored for up to a day. Keep refrigerated and, when ready to serve, grill or pan fry.

Place a tablespoon of spicy fish filling in a line along the center of the rice.

Roll the banana leaf to enclose the rice, then seal the ends with toothpicks.

Banana Custard Surprise

150 g (1$^1/_4$ cups) rice flour

2 tablespoons tapioca flour

500 ml (2$^1/_2$ cups) thin coconut milk

100 g ($^1/_2$ cup) sugar

$^1/_8$ teaspoon salt

2 pandan leaves, torn lengthwise and tied into a knot

2–3 ripe bananas, sliced on the diagonal into 1-cm ($^3/_4$-in) pieces

Banana leaves (or aluminum foil), softened and cut into 18-cm (7-in) squares

Makes 16 cakes
Preparation time: 30 mins
Cooking time: 30 mins

1 Place the rice flour and tapioca flour into a bowl and mix with 200 ml ($^3/_4$ cup) of the thin coconut milk, stirring well to remove any lumps. Set aside.

2 Pour the remaining coconut milk into a saucepan with the sugar, salt and pandan leaves and bring to a boil over medium heat. When the milk comes to a boil, pour in the reserved flour mixture, stirring continuously with a wooden spoon to make a thick, smooth custard.

3 Spoon 2 tablespoons of the custard mixture onto the square of banana leaf or aluminum foil. Place a slice of banana on top of the custard, then spoon another 2 tablespoons onto the banana to enclose it.

4 Shape the custard into an oblong roll and fold the banana leaf around it. Tuck both ends in neatly to make a 6 x 8 cm (2 x 3 in) packet. Arrange the packets in a steamer and steam for 20 minutes. Set aside to cool before serving.

> **Banana leaves** should be passed over an open flame for a few seconds before use to soften them, so that they do not crack when folded. Alternatively, dip the leaves in boiling water until they just start to soften. They are sold in rectangular sheets in supermarkets. If banana leaves are not available, substitute with aluminum foil.

Enclose the banana slice in the rice custard.

Shape the filling into an oblong, then fold the leaf lengthwise.

Palm Sugar Rice Pyramids

200 g (1 cup) glutinous rice, washed and soaked for 3–4 hours (or overnight)

100 g (1 cup) freshly grated coconut

100 g ($^1/_2$ cup) finely chopped palm sugar

$^1/_4$ teaspoon salt

Banana leaves, softened and cut into 18–20 pieces (12 x 12 cm/ 5 x 5 in)

Makes 18–20 cakes
Preparation time: **30 mins + 3 hours soaking**
Cooking time: **25 mins**

1 Drain glutinous rice and grind in a blender to the texture of fine breadcrumbs.

2 In a mixing bowl, combine the ground rice, grated coconut and salt; the mixture should be crumbly.

3 Fold the banana leaf into a wide cone. Fill the tip with 2 tablespoons of the ground rice mixture, hollowing out the middle slightly. Into this hollow, spoon in 1 rounded teaspoon of chopped palm sugar, being careful to enclose it within the ground rice mixture (to prevent leakage during steaming). Top with another scant 1 tablespoon of the ground rice mixture to cover the sugar.

4 Fold the base of the triangle over to enclose neatly and arrange cones on a steamer tray. Steam over medium heat for 25 minutes.

Prepare the ground rice and coconut mixture, the chopped palm sugar, and the leaves.

Fold the banana leaf into a wide cone then fill the tip with some of the rice mixture.

Place some palm sugar into the hollow of the rice mixture then top with a little more rice.

Fold the base of the cone over to enclose the filling then arrange on a steamer tray.

Mashed Banana Coconut Packets

4–5 ripe bananas, mashed to yield 300 g (10 oz)
2 eggs, beaten
50 g ($^1/_4$ cup) sugar
250 ml (1 cup) thick coconut milk
$^1/_4$ teaspoon salt
2 tablespoons powdered milk (optional)
Banana leaves softened and cut into squares and strips (see page 4)
2 large pandan leaves, cut into 5-cm (2-in) lengths

1 Mash bananas and stir in eggs, sugar, thick coconut milk, salt and powdered milk if desired.
2 Take 2 leaf squares for wrapping each cake, stacking one on top of the other. Place a piece of pandan leaf in the center and spoon 3 to 4 tablespoons of the mashed banana mixture onto the leaf. Wrap the cakes according to the instructions on page 4.
3 Steam over medium heat for 20 to 25 minutes, until set. Serve warm or at room temperature.

Makes 15 cakes
Preparation time: **20 mins**
Cooking time: **25 mins**

Sweet Banana Parcels

1 egg
80 g ($^1/_3$ cup) palm sugar, finely chopped
250 ml (1 cup) thick coconut milk
$^1/_4$ teaspoon salt
5 ripe bananas cut into 1-cm ($^1/_2$-in) slices on the diagonal
2 pandan leaves, cut into 5-cm (2-in) lengths
Banana leaves, softened and cut into 15 squares and strips (see page 4)

1 Whisk egg, sugar, coconut milk and salt together until sugar dissolves. Add sliced bananas.
2 Spoon 2 to 3 tablespoons of the banana mixture onto a banana leaf square and wrap according to the instructions on page 4. Arrange parcels in a steamer tray and cook over medium heat for 20 minutes.
3 Unwrap parcels and serve either warm or well chilled.

Makes 15 parcels
Preparation time: **30 mins**
Assembling time: **20 mins**

Place two balls side-by-side on a small piece of pandan leaf on a banana leaf.

Wrap the packet tum-fashion, then add coconut cream just before sealing.

Coconut and Glutinous Rice Flour Cakes

150 ml ($2/3$ cup) thick
  coconut milk
$1/4$ teaspoon salt
Oil for brushing tray
Banana leaves, softened
  and cut into 12 squares
  and strips (see page 4)
3 pandan leaves, cut
  into 4 cm ($1^1/_2$-in)
  lengths

Coconut Filling
175 g ($1^3/4$ cups) young
  grated coconut
125 g ($1/2$ cup +
  1 tablespoon) palm
  sugar, chopped
1 tablespoon sugar
1 drop vanilla essence
$1/4$ teaspoon salt
75 ml ($1/4$ cup +
  2 tablespoons) water

Dough Balls
200 g (2 cups) white
  glutinous rice flour
$1/4$ teaspoon salt
200 ml ($3/4$ cup) coconut
  milk
A few drops red or green
  food coloring (optional)

Makes 12 cakes
Preparation time: **40 mins**
Cooking time: **40 mins**

1 Place the thick coconut milk and salt in a mixing bowl and stir until the salt dissolves. Set aside.

2 Place Coconut Filling ingredients in a saucepan. Cook over medium heat until the mixture is sticky enough to be shaped into balls without disintegrating, about 20 minutes. When cool enough to handle, shape into 24 balls (each about 1 tablespoon). Set aside on a plate.

3 To make Dough Balls, place glutinous rice flour and salt in a mixing bowl. Bring the coconut milk to a boil over medium heat and pour over the flour, mixing well to form a smooth, pliable dough. (If the mixture seems a little dry or crumbly, sprinkle a few drops of warm water over the dough and knead it in.)

4 Divide mixture into two equal parts. Tint one portion either pink or green by kneading in a few drops of food coloring. Leave the remaining portion white. Cover both lots of dough with a clean damp cloth.

5 Lightly brush a baking tray with oil. Roll the uncolored dough into a long roll and pinch off 12 roughly equal-sized pieces. Roll them in your palms to form smooth balls. Arrange on the greased baking tray and cover with a clean damp cloth. Form the colored balls likewise.

6 To fill Dough Balls, place one in the palm of your hand and, using the thumb and forefinger of your other hand, carefully pinch the ball of dough to create a well large enough to accommodate a ball of coconut filling. Pinch the dough around the ball to enclose it completely. Fill all the dough balls this way, returning them on the oiled tray as you make them.

7 To wrap, lightly brush the inside of a banana leaf with oil. Tuck a piece of pandan leaf in the center and arrange two filled balls (one colored and one white) side by side. Fold the parcel according to the instructions on page 4. Before sealing each parcel, carefully pour in 2 tablespoons of coconut milk mixture.

8 Arrange the parcels in a steamer tray and cook over medium heat for 20 minutes. Serve warm or at room temperature.

Sweet Rice and Red Bean Cakes

250 g (1¼ cups) gluti-
nous rice, soaked for
3 hours and drained
3 tablespoons dried
adzuki beans, soaked
for 3 hours and drained
50 g (½ cup) grated
coconut
½ teaspoon salt
14 banana leaves,
softened and cut into
14 x 18 cm (6 x 7 in)
rectangles
String for tying parcels
3 liters (12 cups) water
1 teaspoon salt

Makes 15 parcels
Preparation time: **50 mins
+ 3 hours soaking**
Cooking time: **2 hours**

1 Combine the drained rice, beans, grated coconut and salt in a mixing bowl.
2 Roll 1 banana leaf to form a hollow tube about 2½ cm (1 in) in diameter. Fold one end of the tube.
3 Stand the banana leaf tube on the folded end so the rice does not fall out when you fill the roll. Using a teaspoon, fill each banana leaf tube with rice up to a depth of 7 cm (3 in). Leave about 1 cm (½ in) of space above the fill line and fold this end. Tie each tube with string to prevent rice and beans from leaking out from the tube during cooking.
4 Bring the water to a boil in a large pot and add 1 teaspoon of salt. Slip the rice tubes into the simmering water and cook over medium heat for 1½ to 2 hours. (After 1½ hours, remove one packet and open up to test for doneness. The rice should be firm and compact and the beans tender.) When cooked, remove rice tubes from the water and set aside to drain. Serve warm or at room temperature.

Rice parcels should be covered with water during cooking. If too much water evaporates, leaving the parcels above the water line, top up with more boiling water and continue cooking.

Roll 1 banana leaf to make a hollow tube about 2½ cm (1 in) in diameter.

Fold one end of the tube and stand it on this end.

Fill the tube with rice up to a depth of 7-cm (3-in) and leave 1 cm ($^1/_2$ in) of space at the top.

Tie the tube wih string before cooking.

Form the banana leaf square into a cone shape.

After adding a little coconut cream, fold in the top of the cone to make the base.

Stuffed Rice Flour Cones (Kue Koci)

Banana leaves, softened
and cut into 16 squares
(14 cm/5$^1/_2$-in)
150 ml ($^2/_3$ cup) thick
coconut milk, with a
pinch of salt stirred in

Filling
100 g ($^1/_2$ cup) skinned
dried mung beans
250 ml (1 cup) water
90 g ($^1/_2$ cup) palm
sugar, finely chopped
1 tablespoon sugar
5 tablespoons thick
coconut milk
$^1/_4$ teaspoon salt
Few drops vanilla
essence
1 teaspoon plain flour

Dough
6 large pandan leaves,
cut into 2-cm ($^3/_4$-in)
lengths
150 ml ($^2/_3$ cup) water
1 tablespoon lime water
$^1/_4$ teaspoon salt
150 g (1$^1/_2$ cups) glutinous rice flour
4 tablespoons tapioca
flour or cornflour

Makes 16 cakes
Preparation time: **60 mins**
Cooking time: **40 mins**

1 To make the Filling, wash mung beans in several changes of water. Place in a small pan with 250 ml (1 cup) water. Cook over medium heat until tender and most of the liquid has evaporated. Occasionally stir the pan, to prevent the base from burning.
2 Add both lots of sugar, thick coconut milk, salt and vanilla essence and continue cooking over medium heat until mixture becomes very thick, (10 to 15 minutes). Lastly, sift in the flour and stir quickly to thicken the mixture further; cook for 5 more minutes. Remove from heat and transfer the Filling onto a shallow plate to cool. Use two spoons to shape the Filling into 2$^1/_2$-cm (1-in) balls.
3 To prepare the Dough, place the pandan leaves and water in a blender and process until fine. Strain the mixture and discard any solids to obtain pandan juice. Add the lime water and salt to the pandan juice.
4 Combine the glutinous rice flour and tapioca flour in a mixing bowl. Add the pandan juice, mixing well to form a pliable dough. (If mixture seems dry and crumbly, knead in a few drops of water.) Divide the Dough into 16 equal pieces and shape into balls. Place a ball of Dough in the palm of your hand and, using the thumb and forefinger of your other hand, pinch the Dough to create a well large enough to enclose a ball of Filling. Place the Filling in the well and pinch the Dough to completely enclose the Filling.
5 Lightly brush the inside of a pre-cut sheet of banana leaf and form it into a cone. Place ball of Dough into the cone and carefully pour about 2 teaspoons of thick coconut milk over the ball. Carefully fold the base of the banana leaf, tucking the end in neatly.
6 Arrange the cones in a steamer tray and steam for 20 minutes over medium heat. Set the parcels aside to cool. Unwrap and serve.

Sweet Banana Rice Rolls (Legondo)

250 g (1¹/₄ cups) gluti-
nous rice, soaked for
2 hours and drained
125 ml (¹/₂ cup) coconut
milk
2 pandan leaves,
shredded and tied
into a knot
4 teaspoons sugar
¹/₂ teaspoon salt
Banana leaves, softened
and cut into 24 squares
(15 cm/6 in)
6 ripe bananas, peeled
and halved lengthwise
Cotton string or raffia
for tying up parcels

Makes 12 rolls
Preparation time: **50 mins**
Soaking time: **2–3 hours**
Cooking time: **50 mins**

1 Place drained glutinous rice in a heatproof container
and steam over rapidly-boiling water for 15 minutes.
2 While the rice cooks, place coconut milk, pandan
leaves, sugar and salt in a pan and bring to a boil over
low heat. Once mixture comes to a boil, remove pan
from heat.
3 Pour hot coconut milk over the steamed rice, mixing
well with a wooden spoon until coconut milk is
completely absorbed by the rice.
4 Place 2 sheets of banana leaves on top of each other,
with the sheet facing you glossy side up. Spread 2 to
3 tablespoons of glutinous rice on the banana leaf
and place a halved banana down the center. Enclose
the glutinous rice around the banana, covering it
completely. Roll the banana leaf around the rice and
tuck both ends neatly under. Secure the rolls by tying
string on both ends.
5 Arrange the rolls on a steamer tray and steam for
30 minutes. To serve, untie the string and remove
banana leaves.

Place a halved banana down the center of the glutinous rice.

Roll the banana leaf around the banana, enclosing the rice around the fruit.

Tuck both ends of the roll neatly under.

Secure with string before steaming.

Steamed Sweet Corn Slices

3–4 fresh cobs of corn
300 ml (1 1/4 cups) thick
  coconut milk
2 eggs
70 g (1/3 cup) sugar
2 drops vanilla essence
1 tablespoon cornflour
Banana leaves, softened
  and cut into 12 squares
  and strips (see page 4),
  optional

Makes one 14-cm (6-in)
  cake or 12 parcels
Preparation time: **20 mins**
Cooking time: **30 mins**

1 Using a sharp knife, cut away corn kernels from the cob to yield 300 g (10 oz) corn kernels. Place in a food processor and process until fine. Add the thick coconut milk to the corn and strain.

2 Whisk eggs, sugar and vanilla together until sugar dissolves. Add this to the corn mixture and stir in the cornflour to form a smooth mixture.

3 Pour the mixture into a 14-cm (6-in) shallow cake tin and steam until set, about 30 minutes. Set aside to cool and cut into 3-cm (1 1/4-in) squares or diamonds.

Alternatively, scoop out 3 tablespoons of the corn mixture and place in the center of a large banana sheet wrapper. Wrap according to the instructions on page 4. Repeat until all the corn mixture is used. Steam for 20 minutes, set aside to cool, then unwrap.

Multi-color Layer Cakes

1 liter (4 cups) coconut milk
350 g (1²/₃ cups) sugar
10 kaffir lime leaves
3 pandan leaves, cut into 2-cm (³/₄-in) lengths
550 g (5¹/₂ cups) tapioca flour
A few drops red and yellow food coloring

Makes 30 pieces
Preparation time: **20 mins**
Cooking time: **50 mins**

1 Place coconut milk, sugar, kaffir lime leaves and pandan leaves in a saucepan and bring to a boil. Remove from the heat and set aside to cool slightly.
2 When it is still quite warm, add the tapioca flour and stir until mixture is smooth. Divide batter into 3 equal portions. Leave one portion uncolored. Add a few drops of red food coloring to the second portion of batter and a few drops of yellow food coloring to the third portion of batter.
3 Place a 22-cm (9-in) baking tin in a steamer tray. Pour 3 tablespoons of uncolored batter into the tin and steam for 5 minutes until set. Pour 3 tablespoons of the pink batter over the uncolored layer and steam until set. Pour 3 tablespoons of yellow batter over the pink layer and steam until set. Repeat until all the batter is used, ending with a red layer on top.
4 Steam cake for another 30 minutes. Set aside to cool then remove from the tin. Cut into slices and serve.

Banana Coconut Slices

Bottom Layer
400 ml (1$^2/_3$ cups) thin coconut milk
100 g (scant 1 cup) rice flour
1 tablespoon tapioca flour
125 g ($^1/_2$ cup + 1 tablespoon) sugar
$^1/_4$ teaspoon salt
5–6 ripe bananas, peeled, halved lengthways, sliced in
    1 cm ($^1/_2$ in) pieces on the diagonal

Top Layer
200 ml ($^3/_4$ cup + 1 tablespoon) coconut milk
3 tablespoons rice flour
1 teaspoon sugar
$^1/_4$ teaspoon salt
1 drop vanilla essence

1 To make the Bottom Layer, bring the thin coconut milk to a boil. Remove from the heat and set aside to cool for 5 minutes. Meanwhile, measure rice flour, tapioca flour, sugar and salt into a mixing bowl. Stir to form a smooth mixture. Gradually pour in the hot coconut milk, stirring continuously to obtain a smooth mixture.

2 Stir bananas into the batter. Pour the mixture into a 15-cm (6-in) square baking tin lightly greased with vegetable oil. Steam over medium heat for 20 minutes or until set.

3 Meanwhile, stir all the ingredients for the top layer together and pour this over the base. Continue steaming for another 15 minutes over medium heat, or until the top layer sets.

4 Cool before cutting into squares or diamond shapes.

Makes 20 cakes
Preparation time: **20 mins**
Cooking time: **35 mins**

Rice and Custard Layer Cake

Bottom Rice Layer
450 g (1 lb) uncooked white glutinous rice, soaked
  overnight
1 teaspoon salt
125 ml ($^1/_2$ cup) thick coconut milk
1 pandan leaf, torn lengthwise and tied into a knot

Custard Topping
5 eggs
250 g ($1^1/_4$ cups) finely chopped palm sugar
200 ml ($^3/_4$ cup) thick coconut milk
1 tablespoon rice flour
$^1/_4$ teaspoon salt

1 To make the Bottom Rice Layer, drain the glutinous
rice and place in an 20-cm (8-in) square cake pan.
Add the salt, coconut milk and pandan leaf. Place in a
steamer and steam for 30 minutes or until rice is
cooked. Flake the rice with a fork and press down to
compress it, using a folded sheet of banana leaf or
aluminum foil. Return to the steamer and steam for 5
minutes before adding the Custard Topping.
2 To prepare the Custard Topping, beat the eggs and
sugar in a mixing bowl until the sugar dissolves. Add
the coconut milk and stir in rice flour and salt. Place
the mixing bowl over a saucepan of boiling water and
heat, stirring all the time until the mixture starts to
thicken and coats the back of a spoon. Remove from
the heat immediately and pour over the Bottom Rice
Layer. Steam over low heat for 25 minutes or until
Custard Topping sets.
3 Cool the cake thoroughly before cutting into desired
shapes (slices or diamond shapes).

Makes 15–20 pieces
Preparation time: **30 mins**
Soaking time: **Overnight**
Cooking time: **1 hour**

Place about 2 tablespoons filling into each dough circle.

Fold into a semicircle, pinch down the edges and pleat if desired.

Beef and Vegetable Puffs with Chili Dip

Oil for deep-frying

Filling
100 g ($3^1/_2$ oz) diced
  carrot
100 g ($3^1/_2$ oz) diced
  potatoes
2 tablespoons oil
1 clove garlic, crushed
1 teaspoon white pepper
$^1/_2$ teaspoon salt
200 g (7 oz) lean ground
  beef
100 g (1 cup) bean
  sprouts
1 sprig Chinese celery,
  finely sliced

Pastry
250 g ($2^1/_2$ cups)
  plain flour
$^1/_2$ teaspoon salt
125 ml ($^1/_2$ cup) warm
  water
60 ml ($^1/_2$ cup) oil,
  warmed

Chili Dip
3 red chilies, chopped
5 red bird's-eye chilies
1 clove garlic
5 tablespoons water
1 tablespoon vinegar
$^1/_2$ teaspoon salt
1 tablespoon sugar

Makes 25 pieces
Preparation time: **1 hour**
Cooking time: **40 mins**

1 To make Chili Dip, finely blend all ingredients then tranfer to a small saucepan and bring to a boil. Reduce heat and simmer 5 minutes or until sauce is of desired consistency. Set aside.

2 To make the Filling, place diced carrot in a small saucepan and barely cover with water. Cook for 10 minutes before adding the potato. Cook until both carrot and potato are just tender. Drain in a colander.

3 Heat oil and fry garlic, pepper and salt until fragrant and just beginning to brown. Add minced beef and cook, stirring continuously over high heat until beef is browned. Add carrot and potatoes and stir-fry for 5 minutes before adding the bean sprouts. Cook for 2 minutes, add celery leaves and remove from heat. Transfer to a large shallow plate and set aside to cool.

4 Meanwhile, prepare the Pastry by measuring the flour and salt into a mixing bowl. Make a well in the center. Combine the oil and water and pour into the well, mixing with your fingers to make a firm but pliable dough. Knead for 5 minutes until smooth. Place dough in a bowl, cover with a clean, damp cloth and set aside to rest for 20 minutes before using.

5 Take half the dough and roll out thinly on a lightly-floured working surface. Using a cup or bowl about 9 cm ($3^3/_4$ in) across as a guide, cut Pastry circles with a small sharp knife, keeping them as close together as possible. Gather the Pastry scraps and re-roll. Roll out the remaining Pastry and repeat until you have 25 Pastry circles.

6 Fill each pastry circle with about 2 tablespoons of cooled Filling and fold the edges together to make semi-circular puffs. Press edges together to seal and decorate by pleating edges or pressing down with a fork.

7 Heat 500 to 750 ml (2 to 3 cups) oil in a wok over low to medium heat and slip the filled pastries in the oil. Fry for 3 to 4 minutes per side or until golden brown. Drain on absorbent paper and serve warm, accompanied with the Chili Dip.

Chicken, Prawn and Vegetable Puffs

Oil for deep-frying

Pastry
250 g (2$^1/_2$ cups) plain
  flour
$^1/_2$ teaspoon salt
50 g ($^1/_4$ cup) butter
  or shortening
1 egg, beaten
5 tablespoons water

Filling
60 g (1 oz) diced carrot
5 cloves garlic, crushed
5 shallots, finely minced
1 teaspoon white pepper-
  corns, ground
2 tablespoons butter
100 g (3$^1/_2$ oz) minced
  chicken
70 g (2$^1/_2$ oz) shelled
  prawns, minced
50 g (1$^1/_2$ oz) string or
  French beans, thinly
  sliced on the diagonal
25 g (1 oz) cellophane
  noodles, soaked in hot
  water, drained and cut
  into 5-cm (2-in) lengths
1 tablespoon plain flour
  (for thickening)
3 hard-boiled eggs,
  shelled and cut into
  wedges
2 stalks spring onions
  (scallions), finely sliced
1 stalk Chinese celery,
  finely sliced

Makes 20 pieces
Preparation time: **1 hour**
Cooking time: **40 mins**

1 To make the Pastry, sift flour and salt into a mixing bowl and mix the butter or shortening into the flour until mixture resembles fine breadcrumbs. Beat the egg and water together and add to the flour, a little at a time, until the Pastry comes together. If the mixture seems dry, add a little more water. Knead for a few minutes until smooth and free from cracks. Place in a bowl, cover with a clean, damp cloth and set aside to rest for 15 minutes.

2 To make the Filling, blanch the carrots in boiling water for 8 to 10 minutes until just tender. Drain and set aside.

3 Heat butter in a wok or large skillet and fry the garlic, shallots and pepper until fragrant and lightly browned. Add minced chicken and prawns and stir-fry for 10 minutes before adding the carrots and beans. After 5 minutes, add the drained cellophane noodles, quickly stir-fry and sprinkle over the flour from a sieve. Stir mixture around until thickened and add the spring onions. Remove from heat and transfer the Filling into a large, shallow plate to cool.

4 Divide the Pastry into two equal portions and roll out thinly. Using a cup or bowl about 9 cm (3$^1/_2$ in) across, cut Pastry circles with a small sharp knife, keeping them as close together as possible. Gather the Pastry scraps and re-roll. Roll out the remaining Pastry, until you have 20 circles.

5 Fill each Pastry circle with about 2 tablespoons of cooled Filling and one wedge of hard-boiled egg. Fold the edges to make semi-circular puffs. Press the edges together to seal and decorate by pleating the edges (see page 28) or pressing them down with a fork.

6 Heat oil in a wok or frying pan over medium heat and slip the filled pastries in the oil. Fry each side for 3 to 4 minutes or until golden brown. Drain on kitchen towels and serve warm.

Sugar-frosted Black Rice Cakes

125 g (1¹/₄ cups) black glutinous rice flour
¹/₄ teaspoon salt
50 g (¹/₂ cup) young grated coconut
100 ml (scant ¹/₂ cup) thin coconut milk, warmed
¹/₂ tablespoon slaked lime water
Oil for deep-frying

Sugar Coating
75 g (¹/₃ cup) sugar
2 tablespoons water

Makes 12 cakes
Preparation time: **20 mins**
Cooking time: **20 mins**

1 Combine black glutinous rice flour, salt and grated coconut in a small mixing bowl. Stir together the lime water and warm coconut milk and add to the mixing bowl, mixing with your hands to get a fairly soft, pliable dough. If the dough seems crumbly, knead in a few more drops of water.

2 Knead for a few minutes until smooth and divide dough into 10 to 12 pieces. Roll in your hands into oval shapes and pat them to flatten to about 1 cm (¹/₂ in) thickness.

3 Pour the oil into a wok to a depth of 2¹/₂ cm (1 in). Heat over medium heat and fry the cakes for 3 to 4 minutes on each side. Drain on kitchen towels.

4 To make the Sugar Coating, combine the sugar and water in a small saucepan and bring to a boil over high heat. Simmer until syrup thickens and large bubbles form on its surface. Place cakes in the Sugar Coating and toss the cakes about until the sugar caramelizes on the cakes. Transfer cakes onto a plate and set aside to cool.

These cakes are called 'getas' when made with white glutinous flour and coated with caramelized brown sugar.

Roll the dough in your hands into oval shapes.

Pat the ovals to flatten them to about 1-cm (¹/₂-in) thickness.

Crispy Flower Fritters

100 g (1 cup) rice flour
2 tablespoons sugar
1 egg, beaten
150 ml ($^2/_3$ cup) thin coconut milk
$^1/_4$ teaspoon salt
Oil for deep-frying

1 Mix all ingredients except the oil in a mixing bowl until smooth and free from lumps.
2 Pour the oil into a wok or frying pan to a depth of 4 cm ($1^1/_2$ in). Place a *gembang goyang* mould (see note) in the oil for 4 to 5 minutes. Lift the mould from the oil, letting excess oil drain.
3 Dip hot mould in the batter, up to the level of the mould, to ensure that the batter is easily freed from the mould. Dip the mould into the oil, making sure the mould does not touch the base of the pan. Once the batter hardens slightly, start jiggling the mould gently up and down to free the batter from the mould.
4 Fry the cakes until crisp and golden brown. Remove from the oil and drain on kitchen towels. Repeat the process until all the batter is used up.
5 Set the fritters aside to cool before serving. If not serving immediately, store in an airtight container.

If you do not have the same gembang goyang *mould pictured here, use any shape of metal mould.*

Makes 50 cakes
Preparation time: **10 mins**
Assembling time: **30 mins**

Crispy Sweet Potato Fritters

2–3 sweet potatoes, peeled (about 250 g/8 oz)
50 g ($^1/_4$ cup) palm sugar, finely chopped
$^1/_4$ teaspoon salt
2 teaspoons plain flour
Oil for deep-frying

Batter
4 tablespoons rice flour
1 teaspoon slaked lime water
$^1/_2$ teaspoon sugar
$^1/_4$ teaspoon salt
75 ml ($^1/_3$ cup) water

1 Cut the sweet potatoes into chunks and place in a heatproof dish. Steam over rapidly boiling water until fork tender, about 25 minutes.
2 Mash sweet potatoes until free from lumps. Add sugar, salt and flour to make a dough. Divide the dough into 10 equal portions. Shape each piece to form small patties. Set aside on a plate.
3 To make the Batter, combine the ingredients in a small bowl, stirring well to form a smooth mixture that thinly coats the back of a spoon.
4 Pour the oil into a small wok or saucepan to a depth of 3 cm ($1^1/_4$ in). Heat the oil over medium heat. Dip sweet potato patties into the Batter and fry until crisp and golden brown on all sides. Drain on kitchen towels.

Makes 10 cakes
Preparation time: **20 mins**
Cooking time: **40 mins**

Frosted Rice Flour Fritters

Oil for deep-frying

Dough
175 g (1³/₄ cups) rice flour
¹/₄ teaspoon salt
225 ml (1 cup less 2 tablespoons) very hot water
1 egg yolk, beaten until lighter in color

Sugar Coating
100 g (¹/₂ cup) sugar
4 tablespoons water

Makes 50–60 pieces
Preparation time: **30 mins**
Cooking time: **20 mins**

1 To make the Dough, mix flour and salt in a mixing bowl. Pour over the hot water and continue mixing with a wooden spoon. When cool enough to handle, mix the Dough with your hands and add the egg yolk. Knead to form a smooth dough.

2 Pinch off small pieces of Dough and roll them between your palms to make small elongated pieces, tapered at both ends. Flatten these pieces slightly with your fingers and press down on both sides with the tines of a fork.

3 Pour the oil into a wok to a depth of 3 cm (1¹/₂ in). Heat the oil over medium heat and fry pieces of Dough until crisp and lightly browned. Remove pieces as they are cooked and drain on kitchen towels.

4 To make the Sugar Coating, heat sugar and water in a wok or frying pan until the sugar dissolves. Boil over high heat until syrup is very thick, turns white and starts to crystallize around the edges of the pan. Add the fried fritters and quickly stir them around the pan until coated with the sugar. Remove from pan and set aside to cool. Store in an airtight container if not serving immediately.

In Indonesia, flowers of the areca palm are pressed against the dough for decorative purposes and to help the crystallized sugar to stick.

Pinch off small pieces of dough.

Roll to form small elongated pieces, tapered at both ends.

Flatten the pieces with your fingers.

Press on both sides of the dough with the tines of a fork.

Spicy Tuna Puffs

Dough

1 teaspoon instant yeast
2 tablespoons lukewarm water
250 g (2 cups) plain flour
1 teaspoon salt
1 tablespoon sugar
1 egg, beaten
100 ml (scant $^1/_2$ cup) thin coconut milk
Oil for greasing

Filling

1 tablespoon lime juice
200 g ($6^1/_2$ oz) tuna fillet (boned weight)
3 large red chilies
5 red bird's-eye chilies
1 cm ($^1/_2$ in) ginger, chopped
3 shallots
2 cloves garlic
3 tablespoons oil
1 medium tomato, diced
1 pandan leaf, finely shredded
5 kaffir lime leaves, finely shredded
20–30 lemon basil leaves (*daun kemangi*), shredded
250 ml (1 cup) thick coconut milk
$^1/_4$ teaspoon salt
$^1/_2$ teaspoon sugar

Serves 4
Preparation time: **50 mins**
Rising time: **1 hour 40 mins**
Cooking time: **40 mins**

1 To make the Dough, sprinkle yeast onto the lukewarm water and set aside for 15 minutes until frothy. Combine flour, salt and sugar in a mixing bowl and make a well in the center. Into the well, pour the yeast mixture, beaten egg and thin coconut milk. Mix with your hands to form a soft Dough. Turn the Dough out onto a lightly-floured surface and knead until smooth and elastic, about 15 minutes. Lightly oil a bowl and place the Dough in it. Cover bowl with a damp cloth and leave to rise at room temperature until the Dough doubles in size, about $1^1/_2$ hours.

2 To make the Filling, squeeze lime juice over the fish and marinate for 10 minutes before steaming over high heat for 20 minutes. When cool enough to handle, remove skin and bones. Flake finely.

3 While the fish is steaming, grind both lots of chilies, ginger, shallots and garlic together in an electric blender. Add a little water if needed to keep the mixture turning. Set aside. Heat oil in a wok and fry ground ingredients and diced tomatoes over low heat until fragrant and oil separates. Add the fish, shredded herbs and thick coconut milk. Simmer until Filling is quite dry. Season with salt and sugar and stir-fry for a few more minutes. Transfer onto a plate to cool.

4 Turn Dough out of the bowl and knead for a few minutes on a lighly-floured surface. Form into a long roll and cut off 16 equal portions.

5 Roll each piece into a smooth ball and set aside. Cover with a damp cloth to prevent a thin crust forming on the surface of the Dough. Flatten each ball of Dough and fill with the cooled Filling. Fold the circle to enclose the Dough to form a semicircle shape. Press and crimp the edges.

6 Arrange shaped pastries on a lightly-oiled baking tray and set aside to rise for 10–15 minutes.

7 Pour the oil in a wok to a depth of 4 cm ($1^1/_2$ in). Heat over medium heat. Slip the filled Dough pieces into the hot oil. Fry each piece for 2 to 3 minutes on each side or until golden brown. Drain on kitchen towels and serve warm.

Steamed Pandan Cakes in Palm Sugar Syrup

5 large pandan leaves
100 ml (scant $^1/_2$ cup)
  water
250 g ($2^1/_2$ cups) white
  glutinous rice flour
$^1/_2$ teaspoon salt
1 teaspoon slaked lime
  water
125 ml ($^1/_2$ cup) water
2 pieces banana leaf (for
  lining steaming tray)
Oil for greasing banana
  leaf
100 g (1 cup) grated
  coconut
$^1/_4$ teaspoon salt

Palm Sugar Syrup
100 g ($^1/_2$ cup) palm
  sugar, finely chopped
$3^1/_2$ tablespoons water
1 pandan leaf, torn
  lengthwise and tied in
  a knot

Serves 4
Preparation time: **40 mins**
Cooking time: **30 mins**

1 Cut pandan leaves into 2-cm ($^3/_4$-in) lengths and place in a food processor with 100 ml of water and process finely. Strain and discard solids to obtain pandan juice.

2 Place flour and salt in a bowl and pour in the pandan juice, slaked lime water and enough additional water to form a smooth, pliable dough. If the dough feels crumbly to the touch, add a few more drops of water. Knead dough for a few minutes.

3 Line the base of a shallow cake tin with a banana leaf (cut to fit). Lightly grease the leaf with oil to prevent the cakes from sticking.

4 To shape cakes, pinch off small pieces of dough and roll into smooth balls, about $2^1/_2$ cm (1 in) across. Flatten the dough to a thickness of 1 cm ($^1/_2$ in) and press the centers to create a slight depression.

5 Arrange the button-shaped cakes on the oiled banana leaves, spaced at least 2 cm ($^3/_4$ in) away from each other, to ensure that they do not stick together. Place in a steamer and steam for 15 to 20 minutes.

6 While the cakes are steaming, make the Palm Sugar Syrup by boiling the chopped palm sugar, water and pandan leaf together until the sugar dissolves and the syrup is slightly thick and sticky. Strain into a small jug or bowl.

7 Combine the grated coconut and salt in a separate bowl and steam for 15 minutes.

8 To serve, sprinkle the grated coconut over the cakes and drizzle the Palm Sugar Syrup over.

Roll the dough into smooth balls the size of small limes.

Press the center of each ball to create a slight depression.

Coconut Cakes with Palm Sugar Syrup

100 g (1 cup) freshly
  grated coconut
$1/4$ teaspoon salt

Dough
200 g (2 cups) white
  glutinous rice flour
5 tablespoons tapioca
  flour
$1/4$ teaspoon salt
100 ml (scant $1/2$ cup)
  water

Palm Sugar Syrup
200 g (1 cup) palm
  sugar, finely chopped
120 ml ($1/2$ cup) water

Serves 4
Preparation time: **40 mins**
Cooking time: **30 mins**

1 Mix the grated coconut and salt together and steam for 15 minutes. Set aside.

2 To prepare the Palm Sugar Syrup, place palm sugar and water in a small pan and simmer until mixture is slightly thick and sticky. Strain into a small jug or bowl and set aside.

3 To make the Dough, combine the glutinous rice flour, tapioca flour and salt in a mixing bowl. Add enough water to form a soft, pliable dough. If dough seems crumbly, add a few drops of water.

4 Pinch off pieces of dough and roll them between your palms into thin cylinders. Slice into 1 cm ($1/2$ in) pieces on the diagonal.

5 Bring a pan of water to a boil over medium heat. Working in batches, gently drop the cakes into the boiling water. When they rise to the surface, indicating that they are cooked, remove them with a slotted spoon and roll them in the grated coconut.

6 Serve drizzled with the Palm Sugar Syrup.

Roll the dough into cylinders the width of your forefinger, then cut into diagonal slices.

Roll the cakes in the grated coconut.

Bananas in a Blanket with Coconut Cream

7–8 cooking bananas (*pisang kapok* or *pisang raja*)

5–6 pandan leaves, each cut into 2 cm ($3/_4$ in) lengths

100 ml (scant $1/_2$ cup) water

2–3 drops green food coloring (optional)

150 g ($1^1/_2$ cups) rice flour

5 tablespoons plain flour

350 ml (scant $1^1/_2$ cups) thin coconut milk

75 g ($1/_3$ cup plus 2 tablespoons) sugar

Coconut Cream Sauce

500 ml (2 cups) thick coconut milk

5 tablespoons rice flour

100 g (1 cup less 2 tablespoons) plain flour

$1/_4$ teaspoon salt

2 drops vanilla essence

Serves 4
Preparation time: **1 hour**
Cooking time: **40 mins**

1 Steam the bananas in their skins for 5 to 7 minutes. Set aside to cool.

2 Place the pandan leaves and water in a food processor and process finely. Strain and discard solids to obtain pandan juice. Add a few drops of green food coloring if desired.

3 Combine the pandan juice, rice flour, plain flour, thin coconut milk and sugar in a saucepan, stirring to form a smooth mixture. Cook over low heat, stirring continuously until mixture forms a dough that leaves the sides of the pan clean. Remove pan from heat. When cool enough to handle, knead the warm dough until smooth.

4 To shape the cakes, place 2 to 3 tablespoons of dough on a lightly oiled banana leaf, about 18 cm (7 in) square. Flatten the dough to a thickness of $1/_2$ cm ($1/_4$ in) and place a whole, peeled, steamed banana in the center of the dough. Carefully fold the dough over the banana to enclose it completely. As far as possible, conceal any joints by smoothing and patting the dough over the seams. Add a stalk at one end of the banana—the final appearance should be that of an unpeeled banana complete with stalk.

5 Place the "bananas" in a shallow heatproof dish that has been lightly oiled and steam cakes for 15 minutes.

6 Meanwhile, combine the ingredients for the Coconut Cream Sauce in a small saucepan. When smooth and free from lumps, cook over gentle heat until sauce boils and thickens.

7 To serve, cut the "bananas" into thin slices on the diagonal and pour over the Coconut Cream Sauce.

Ground Almond Cakes

150 ml ($^2/_3$ cup) water
150 g ($^3/_4$ cup) sugar
3 egg yolks
1 drop vanilla essence

Dough
2–3 medium potatoes (about 250 g/8 oz)
50 g ($^1/_2$ cup) ground almonds
50 g ($^1/_4$ cup) sugar

1 To make the Dough, scrub potatoes and boil until tender. Peel and mash until free from lumps. Combine the mashed potatoes with the ground almonds and 50 g ($^1/_4$ cup) of sugar. If the Dough seems a little soft, place mixture in a small pan and cook over low heat for a few minutes to dry it out until it becomes pliable.
2 Pinch off small pieces of Dough and roll each piece into slightly elongated balls so they look like jackfruit seeds. Place "seeds" on a tray, ready to be poached.
3 Pour water and 150 g ($^3/_4$ cup) of sugar in a small pan and heat gently until sugar dissolves and the mixture is syrupy.
4 Beat egg yolks and vanilla essence. Dip the Dough balls into the egg yolk. Lift the Dough balls from the egg yolk mixture one at a time and place in the syrup. Poach gently for a few minutes until the egg yolk sets and forms a frilly coating around the Dough ball. Remove with a slotted spoon and continue poaching the rest of the Dough balls in the syrup.
5 Serve in a bowl drizzled with a little leftover syrup. Serve cold or at room temperature.

Serves 4
Preparation time: **30 mins**
Cooking time: **40 mins**

Sweet Mung Bean Patties

4–5 banana leaf sheets, softened

Filling
200 g (1 cup) skinned mung beans
800 ml (3^1/$_4$ cups) water
200 g (1 cup) sugar
2 drops vanilla essence
100 ml (scant ^{1}/$_2$ cup) coconut milk

Dough
250 ml (1 cup) coconut milk
250 g (2^1/$_2$ cups) glutinous rice flour
75 g (^{1}/$_3$ cup) sugar
^{1}/$_2$ teaspoon salt

Serves 4
Preparation time: **40 mins**
Cooking time: **1 hour**

1 To make the Filling, rinse mung beans in several changes of water. Place in a pan with the water and cook over medium heat for about 30 minutes, or until beans are completely soft and disintegrated and most of the liquid evaporates. Add the sugar, vanilla essence and coconut milk and continue cooking until the mixture is thick and pulpy, 10–15 minutes. Transfer Filling into a shallow plate to cool.

2 To make the Dough, bring the coconut milk to a boil over medium heat. Combine the rice flour, sugar and salt in a mixing bowl and pour over the hot coconut milk, stirring with a spoon and then kneading with your hands when it is cool enough to handle. Knead to form a soft, pliable dough. If the mixture is too soft, knead in 1 to 2 more tablespoons of glutinous rice flour.

3 Cut out 25 to 30 circles of banana leaves just slightly larger than the base of your *kue ku* mould (see picture on page 51).

4 To shape cakes, take 1 tablespoon of Dough and roll into a smooth ball. Flatten until about ^{1}/$_2$ cm (^{1}/$_4$ in) thick and place a tablespoon of Filling in the center. Pinch the Dough around the Filling to enclose it.

5 Press the Dough firmly into the mould. Carefully ease the Dough from the edges of the mould with your fingers. Turn the mould upside down and give it a sharp tap on your table top—the Dough should come out from the mould with the design of the mould embossed on it. Turn the Dough over the right side up and place its base on one banana leaf circle.

6 Arrange Dough on a steamer tray and steam over medium heat for 20 minutes. Serve warm or at room temperature.

If you do not have the same kue ku *mould pictured here, use any depressed mould that will emboss an interesting pattern onto the cake.*

Place the Filling in the center of the Dough circle, then pinch the Dough close.

Press the Dough firmly into the mould.

Steamed Caramel Cakes

200 g (1 cup) sugar
100 ml (scant $^1/_2$ cup) water
5 tablespoons powdered milk
200 g (1$^2/_3$ cups) flour
$^1/_2$ teaspoon bicarbonate of soda
4 eggs
6 tablespoons sugar
100 g (1 cup) grated coconut
$^1/_4$ teaspoon salt

1 Place sugar in a saucepan and melt over medium heat until it caramelizes and turns golden brown. Add water to the pan and bring to a boil. Simmer for 5 to 7 minutes over medium heat until caramel dissolves completely and mixture is syrupy. Set aside to cool.
2 Sift powdered milk, flour and bicarbonate of soda together. Set aside. Place small heatproof moulds in the tray, leaving them to heat as you mix the batter.
3 Whisk eggs and sugar together until light and fluffy. Using a spatula, fold the sifted flour into the syrup and then fold in the beaten eggs, being careful not to overwork the mixture or it will lose volume.
4 Fill the moulds three-quarters full with the mixture and steam for 8 to 12 minutes, depending on the size and depth of the moulds.
5 Set cakes aside to cool before removing them from the moulds. Mix the grated coconut and salt together and top each cake with a little coconut before serving.

Makes 10–15 cakes
Preparation time: **20 mins**
Cooking time: **15 mins**

Baked Coconut and Tapioca Cakes

150 g ($^3/_4$ cup)
  margarine or butter
300 g (1$^1/_2$ cups) sugar
2 egg yolks
400 g (4 cups) freshly
  grated coconut flesh
  (white part only)
400 g (4 cups) tapioca
  flour
$^1/_4$ teaspoon salt
$^1/_4$ teaspoon vanilla
  essence

Serves 4
Preparation time: **15 mins**
Cooking time: **50 mins**

1 Preheat oven to 175°C (340°F) and grease a shallow baking tray measuring 21 x 30 cm (8$^1/_2$ x 12 in).
2 Beat margarine or butter with the sugar and vanilla essence until light and fluffy. Beat in the yolks, one at a time. Stir in coconut, flour and salt, mixing well to form a very firm mixture.
3 Pat mixture into the prepared tin, leveling the top. Using a knife, mark out 4 x 6 cm (1$^3/_4$ x 2$^1/_2$ in) rectangles onto the surface of the mixture. Bake in preheated oven for 40 to 50 minutes or until golden brown and crisp.
4 Cut the cake into slices, following the pre-marked lines. Place on 2 baking trays and bake for a second time in the oven for 15 to 20 minutes or until crisp. Set aside to cool and store in an airtight container.

Spiced Sponge Cakes

350 ml (scant 1^1/$_2$ cups) coconut milk
5 pandan leaves
100 ml (scant ^{1}/$_2$ cup) water
250 g (1^1/$_4$ cups) plain flour
1 teaspoon ground fennel
^{1}/$_4$ teaspoon ground nutmeg
1 teaspoon ground cinnamon
3 eggs
200 g (1 cup) sugar
^{1}/$_4$ teaspoon vanilla essence

1 Bring the coconut milk to a boil over low heat. Remove pan from the heat and set aside to cool.
2 Cut pandan leaves into 2 cm (^{3}/$_4$ in) lengths and place in a food processor with the water. Blend until smooth, then strain and discard solids to obtain pandan juice. Sift flour and spices together. Set aside.
3 Preheat oven to 175°C (340°F). Line the base of a cake tin measuring 15 cm (6 in) across with greaseproof paper and grease lightly.
4 Whisk eggs and sugar until mixture is light and thick. Fold in the sifted flour, a few tablespoons at a time, alternately with the pandan juice and coconut milk. Pour batter into the cake tin and bake for 30 to 40 minutes or until top is golden brown.

Serves 4
Preparation time: **40 mins**
Cooking time: **40 mins**

Durian Cookies

Filling

300 g (10 oz) seeded durian flesh

75 g ($^1/_3$ cup) finely chopped palm sugar

2 tablespoons white granulated sugar

Pastry

200 g (1 cup) butter

3 tablespoons icing sugar

2 egg yolks

300 g ($2^1/_2$ cups) flour

1 tablespoon water

1 egg yolk, beaten, for glazing

Serves 4

Preparation time: **1 hour**

Cooking time: **40 mins**

1 To make the Filling, place durian and both lots of sugar in a small, heavy-based saucepan. Cook over low heat, stirring constantly to prevent the base from burning, until mixture becomes thick and sticky, about 25 minutes. Transfer Filling into a shallow plate and set aside to cool completely.

2 To make the Pastry, beat butter and sugar together in a mixing bowl until creamy. Add the yolks and continue beating until light and fluffy. Stir in the flour with a metal spoon or spatula, adding a few drops of water if the mixture looks crumbly.

3 Scoop 1 tablespoon of the Pastry and roll into a ball. Form a well in the center and place a teaspoon of Filling. Carefully pinch Pastry to enclose Filling. Arrange filled pastries 2 cm ($^3/_4$ in) apart on a lightly buttered baking tray.

4 Preheat an oven to 180°C (350°F).

5 If desired, make shallow cuts around each piece of Pastry so it resembles a durian (see picture on page 57). Lightly brush pastries with egg yolk and bake in the preheated oven for 15 to 17 minutes or until pastries are crisp and very lightly browned. Set aside to cool before storing in an airtight container.

Roll Dough into a ball and make a 'well' in the center.

Place the Filling into the 'well'.

Carefully pinch the pastry to enclose the Filling.

Make shallow cuts around the cake so that it resembles a durian.

Baked Coconut Custard

5 young green coconuts
100 ml (scant $^1/_2$ cup)
  sweetened condensed
  milk
125 ml ($^1/_2$ cup) water
6 egg yolks
$^1/_4$ teaspoon vanilla
  essence
6 tablespoons sugar
50 g (scant $^1/_2$ cup) flour

Topping
4 egg whites
1 tablespoon sugar
$^1/_4$ teaspoon salt
50 g (1$^1/_2$ oz) raisins

Serves 4
Preparation time: **5 mins**
Cooking time: **5 mins**

1 Scrape the flesh from the coconut and cut into small dice. Set aside. Preheat oven to 160°C (325°F).
2 Combine the milk and water in a saucepan and place over low heat. Whisk egg yolks, vanilla essence and sugar together until thick and light-colored. Fold in the flour and pour the hot milk into the egg yolk mixture, stirring well. Return mixture to the pan and cook until the custard thickens. Add coconut flesh.
3 Pour coconut mixture into a bowl and set aside.
4 To make the Topping, whisk the egg whites, sugar and salt in a clean, dry bowl until stiff. Spread this over the coconut mixture and sprinkle over the raisins. Bake in the preheated oven until Topping sets and the surface is golden brown, about 20 minutes.
5 Serve warm or at room temperature.

This dessert cannot be cut into pieces, but should be spooned into serving dishes.

Durian Cake

Butter or margarine, softened (for greasing)
Flour for dusting
175 ml ($^3/_4$ cup) thick
coconut milk
350 g (1$^1/_2$ oz) seeded
durian flesh
3 eggs
200 g (1 cup) sugar
250 g (2 cups) flour

Serves 4
Preparation time: **30 mins**
Cooking time: **50 mins**

1 Lightly grease a 15-cm (6-in) cake tin with softened butter or margarine. Dust lightly with a little flour and tap out excess. Preheat an oven to 175°C (340°F).
2 Bring the coconut milk to a boil over low heat in a small saucepan. Set aside to cool, then combine it with the durian flesh. Mix well.
3 Whisk eggs and sugar together until thick and light-colored. Using a large metal spoon or rubber spatula, fold in the flour and durian mixture alternately, in three or four batches. When both ingredients have been incorporated, stop mixing and turn batter into the prepared tin.
4 Bake in the preheated oven for 30 to 40 minutes or until cake is golden brown and a skewer inserted in the middle comes out clean. Set aside to cool before cutting into small serving pieces.

Rice Flour Biscuits

125 g (1¹/₄ cups) grated coconut
300 g (3 cups) rice flour
150 g (1¹/₂) cups starch of the aren palm or tapioca flour
¹/₂ teaspoon bicarbonate of soda
1 teaspoon ground cinnamon
¹/₄ teaspoon ground nutmeg
Butter or oil for greasing
3 whole eggs
1 egg yolk
175 g (1³/₄ cups) sugar
125 g (³/₄ cup) palm sugar, finely chopped
Tapioca flour for dusting

Serves 4
Preparation time: **40 mins**
Cooking time: **50 mins**

1 Place grated coconut in a wok or frying pan and dry fry over low heat, stirring constantly to prevent burning. Cook until coconut is golden brown, about 20 minutes. Remove from the heat and set aside to cool slightly before grinding in a spice grinder. Grind the coconut until it is fine and exudes oil. Set aside.
2 Wipe wok or pan dry and dry fry the rice flour and aren starch or tapioca flour over low heat until the flour feels light and dry, about 10 minutes. Set aside to cool. Stir in the bicarbonate of soda, ground cinnamon, nutmeg and coconut.
3 Preheat oven to 180°C (350°F). Lightly brush 2 to 3 baking trays with butter or oil.
4 Whisk the eggs, egg yolk and both lots of sugar together with an electric beater until mixture is thick and light. Fold half the dry fried ingredients into the mixture, using a large metal spoon or spatula. Fold in the remainder until the dough binds together. Knead gently on a lightly floured surface.
5 Working with one-third of the dough at a time, roll mixture out on a working surface lightly dusted with tapioca flour. Roll out evenly with a rolling pin to a thickness of ¹/₂ cm (¹/₄ in). Stamp out biscuits using a cookie cutter dipped in flour.
6 Lift biscuits onto prepared trays, arranging them 1 cm (¹/₂ in) apart. Bake in a preheated oven for 12 to 15 minutes or until lightly colored and crisp to the touch. Set aside to cool, then store in an airtight container.

Stamp out the biscuits with a cookie cutter.

Arrange biscuits on the lightly greased trays about 1 cm (¹/₂ in) apart.

Iced Fruit Cocktail

400 g (13 oz) ripe avocado, cut into 1-cm ($^1/_2$-in) cubes
400 g (13 oz) ripe jackfruit, seeded and cut into
  1-cm ($^1/_2$-in) cubes
3 young coconuts, white flesh scraped out
Crushed ice
Condensed milk to taste

Syrup
150 g ($1^1/_2$ cups) sugar
2 pandan leaves, shredded lengthwise and tied in
  a knot
$3^1/_2$ tablespoons (50 ml) water

1 To make the Syrup, combine sugar, pandan leaves and water in a small saucepan and heat for a few minutes over low heat until sugar dissolves. Set aside to cool.
2 To serve, place spoonfuls of cubed avocado, jackfruit and young coconut flesh into a serving bowl. Add a little Syrup to sweeten, top with crushed ice and drizzle on a little condensed milk. Serve immediately.

Serves 4–6
Preparation time: **30 mins**

Index